A Pocketful of Saki

~The Savage Wit of H. H. Munro~

*Selected from the stories, plays,
and other works*

*Edited
by
John Pidgeon*

A Pocketful of Saki:
The Savage Wit of H. H. Munro

This selection copyright © 2022 John Pidgeon
All rights reserved.

ISBN: 978-1-957453-02-6 (paperback)
ISBN: 978-1-957453-03-3 (e-book)
Library of Congress Control Number: 2022907376

Big Woods Publications
Green Bay, Wisconsin

BigWoodsPublications@Outlook.com
www.BigWoodsPublications.wix.com/Books

Printed in the United States of America.

Nobody else is quite like him. He has had no successful imitators, and he imitated no one. His writing is the perfection of high-bred malice, a malice without ugliness.
— Robertson Davies

The victims are sufficiently foolish to awaken no sympathy — they are the middle-aged, the people with power; it is right that they should suffer a temporary humiliation because the world is always on their side in the long run. Munro, like a chivalrous highwayman, robs only the rich: behind all these stories is an exacting sense of justice.

— Graham Greene

His whimsicality and wit, his wonderful sense of irony, his profound understanding of people (especially children), and his ability to satirize human weakness with urbane malice and charm all qualify him for his unique place among the great storytellers.
— Richard Corbin

There is no mystery about the continued popularity of Saki's stories. They make us laugh, they up-end respectability, and they provide unflagging entertainment. The deftness of their wit and the ingenuity of their anecdotes are as effective as ever. His satire is still relevant.
— J. W. Lambert

[The stories] remain because they are so much more than funny.
— Tom Sharpe

Delight, gentle reader, in his ability to render the sensate in terms of the insensate, as when he compares the soul to a drawing room, or comments on the pain threshold of toast. Titter nervously as he avers that the oyster is more beautiful than any religion. And gasp as your expectations are not so much reversed as sent into free fall.
— Will Self

He employed successfully a wildly outrageous premise in order to make a serious point. And today the best of his stories are still better than the best of just about every other writer around.
— Roald Dahl

Looking back, I realize that one of the most significant influences on my career as a writer was Saki. His stories remain as delightful and sophisticated as when first published. They are dated only in that they describe a society that vanished in the baleful summer of 1914.

— Noel Coward

There is no greater compliment to be paid the right kind of friend than to hand him Saki, without comment.
— Christopher Morley

Introductory Note

Hector Munro, who published under the penname Saki, was a Briton born in Colonial Burma in 1870. Forty-six years later, in 1916, he perished in a shallow crater near the front in the midst of WWI. His last words: "Put that bloody cigarette out!"

In between these dates he published the prose works from which this selection has been made. Slight emendations exist where archaic usage or the out-of-context nature of a quotation may call for it.

Saki was the quintessential satirist of Edwardian manners, displaying an almost vicious sensibility in his castigation of pretentious class-conscious niceties. A near-contemporary of Oscar Wilde, Munro wrote some of the finest short stories of wit and humor in the language. You will enjoy making his nearer acquaintance.

— John Pidgeon

Contents

A Pocketful of Saki 1

For Further Reading 99

Appendix A: *A List of the Indispensable Tales* . . 101

Appendix B: *A Saki Nomenclature* 102

A Pocketful of Saki

*from **Reginald**, a collection of stories & sketches*:

"People may say what they like about the decay of Christianity," said Reginald, "but the religious system that produced green Chartreuse can never really die."

I think she must have been very strictly brought up, she's so desperately anxious to do the wrong thing correctly.

"If you're going to be rude," said Reginald, "I shall dine with you tomorrow night as well."

The doctors said at the time that she couldn't live more than a fortnight, and she's been trying ever since to see if she could. Women are so opinionated.

They tried to rag me in the smoking room about not being able to hit a bird at five yards, a sort of bovine ragging that suggested cows buzzing round a gadfly and thinking they were teasing it.

So, I got up the next morning at dawn — I know it was dawn because the grass looked as if it had been left out all night.

To be clever in the afternoon argues that one is dining nowhere in the evening.

Reginald affects an exhaustive knowledge of things political, which furnishes an excellent excuse for not discussing them.

"When I was at Poona in '76 —"
"My dear Colonel," purred Reginald, "fancy admitting such a thing! Such a giveaway of one's age! I wouldn't admit being on this planet in '76." Reginald in his wildest lapses into veracity would never admit to being more than twenty-two.

Reginald was engaged in teaching the youngest Rampage boy the approved theory for mixing absinthe [a notorious liqueur] within full earshot of his mother. Mrs. Rampage occupies a prominent place in local temperance movements.

Reginald is discussing *Zaza* [a controversial stage production] with the Archdeacon's wife. At least, he is discussing; she is ordering her carriage.

I found everyone talking nervously and feverishly of the weather and the war in South Africa, except Reginald, who was reclining now in a comfortable chair with the dreamy, faraway look that a volcano might wear after it had desolated entire villages.

There were symptoms of a stampede [at the dinner party]. The Archbishop's wife looked at me. Kipling or someone has described somewhere the look that a foundering camel gives when the caravan moves on and leaves it to its fate. The peptonized reproach in the good lady's eyes brought the passage vividly to mind.

She spoke in the dry, staccato tone of one who repeats a French lesson.

There is, for instance, the female relative in the country who "knows a tie is always useful" and sends you some spotted horror that you could only wear in secret or in Tottenham Court Road. It is an admitted fact that the ordinary tomtit of commerce has a sounder aesthetic taste than the average female relative in the country.

She comes from the North, where they live in fear of Heaven and the Earl of Durham.

I hate posterity — it's so fond of having the last word.

"Every reformation must have its victims," put in Reginald. "You can't expect the fatted calf to share the enthusiasm of the angels over the prodigal's return."

I must confess that such persons make me feel uncomfy; they remind one so of a duck that goes flapping about with forced cheerfulness long after its head's been cut off.

"Of course," resumed the Duchess combatively, "it's the prevailing fashion to believe in perpetual change and mutability and all that sort of thing, and to say we are all merely an improved form of primeval ape — of course you subscribe to that doctrine?"

"I think it decidedly premature," said Reginald. "In most people I know the process is far from complete."

"And equally of course you are quite irreligious?"

"Oh, by no means. The fashion just now is [to have] a Roman Catholic frame of mind with an Agnostic conscience: you get the medieval picturesqueness of the one with the modern conveniences of the other."

"Never," said Reginald, "be a pioneer. It's the early Christian who gets the fattest lion."

"After all," said the Duchess, "there are certain things you can't get away from. Right and wrong, good conduct and moral rectitude have certain well-defined limits."

"So, for that matter," replied Reginald, "has the Russian Empire. The trouble is that the limits are not always in the same place."

The thing is to say what everyone else is saying, only to say it better.

"Your philanthropy," said, Reginald, "practiced in a world where everything is based on competition, must have a debit as well as a credit account. Young ravens must be fed."

"And are fed," said the Countess.

"Exactly. Which presumes that something else is fed upon."

"Oh, you're simply exasperating. You've been reading Nietzsche till you haven't got any sense of moral proportion left. When I was younger, boys your age used to be nice and innocent."

"Now we are only nice," said Reginald. "One must specialize these days."

The family ate porridge and believed in everything, even the weather forecast.

The reason one's elders know so comparatively little is because they have to unlearn so much that they acquired by way of education before we were born. To my mind, education is an absurdly overrated affair. At least one never took it very seriously at school, where everything was done to bring it prominently under one's notice.

There was a fellow I stayed with once in Warwickshire who farmed his own land, but was otherwise quite steady.

As I said to Lady Beauwhistle, if you want a lesson in elaborate artificiality, just watch the studied unconcern of a Persian cat entering a crowded salon, and then go practice it for two weeks.

Her frocks are made in Paris, but she wears them with a strong English accent.

She believed in the healthy influence of natural surroundings, never having been to Sicily.

Just when I was doing my best to understand half the things I was saying . . .

One likes to escape from oneself occasionally.

"Someone has observed that Providence is always on the side of the big dividends," remarked Reginald. The Duchess ate her anchovy in a shocked manner; she was sufficiently old-fashioned enough to dislike irreverence towards dividends.

They charge so much for excess baggage on some of those foreign lines that it's really an economy to leave one's reputation behind one occasionally.

The young have aspirations that never come to pass, the old have reminiscences of what never happened. It's only the middle-aged who are really conscious of their limitations.

It's not always safe to depend on the commemorative tendencies of those who come after us. There may have been disillusionments in the lives of the saints, but they would scarcely have been better pleased if they could have foreseen that their names would be associated chiefly with racehorses and the cheaper clarets.

"There was once a woman who told the truth," said Reginald. "Not all at once of course, but the habit grew on her. It began with little things, for no particular reason except that her life was a rather empty one, and it is so easy to slip into the habit of telling the truth in little matters."

The cook was a good cook, as cooks go; and as cooks go, she went.

No really provident woman lunches regularly with her husband if she wishes to burst upon him as a revelation at dinner. He must have time to forget; an afternoon is not enough.

Reginald closed his eyes with the elaborate weariness of one who has rather nice eyelashes and thinks it useless to conceal the fact.

When the liqueur began to take effect, she started to give them imitations of animals. She began with a dancing bear, and then she got up on the piano and gave them an organ monkey. I gather she went in for realism rather than a Maeterlinckian treatment of the subject.

There are only two classes that really can't help taking life seriously — schoolgirls of thirteen and Hohenzollerns, and they might be exempt. Albanians come under another heading; they take life whenever they get the opportunity.

As we were coming home through some meadows, she made a quite unnecessary attempt to see if her pony would jump a rather messy brook. It wouldn't. I had to fish her out from the bank.

What exactly is a raw commodity? Mrs. Van Challaby says that men are raw commodities until you marry them.

She said things about me which in her calmer moments she would have hesitated to spell.

Mrs. Babwold wears a rather solemn personality, and has never been known to smile, even when saying disagreeable things to her friends.

When a man goes out in the pouring rain to brush caterpillars off rose trees, I generally imagine his life indoors leaves something to be desired. Anyway, it must be very unsettling for the caterpillars.

The Major turned a beautiful Tyrian scarlet, and I remember thinking at the time that I should like my bathroom done in that color.

She asked him why he didn't publish a book of his sporting reminiscences; it would be *so* interesting. She didn't remember till afterwards that he had given her two fat volumes on the subject, with his portrait and autograph as a front piece.

Then the Major gave us a graphic account of his struggle with a wounded bear. I privately wished that the bear would win sometimes on these occasions; at least he wouldn't go vaporizing about it afterwards.

It was decorated with Japanese fans and Chinese lanterns, which gave it a very Old English effect.

There was a note pinned to her door with a signed request that she be called particularly early on the morrow. Reginald covered up everything except the signature with another note, to the effect that before these words should meet the eye, she would have ended a misspent life, was sorry for the trouble she was giving, and would like a military funeral.

The [mind-reader] was rather a success; he announced that she was thinking about poetry, and she admitted that her mind was dwelling on one of Austin's odes, which was near enough.

The Duchess gave me a pamphlet to leave at the house of a doubtful voter, and some grapes and jellies for a woman suffering from a chill. I thought it much cleverer to give the grapes and things to the former and the political literature to the sick woman. The Duchess was quite absurdly annoyed about it afterwards. It seems the leaflet was addressed, "To those about to wobble" — I wasn't responsible for the silly title of the thing — and the woman never recovered. Anyway, the voter was completely won over by the grapes and jellies, and I think that should have balanced things.

"Youth," said the other, "should suggest innocence."

"But never act on the suggestion," said Reginald. "People talk vaguely about the innocence of a little child, but they take mighty good care not to let it out of their sight for twenty minutes."

She said it wasn't Persian enough, as though I were trying to sell her a kitten whose mother had married for love rather than pedigree.

"I'd like to write a book of personal reminiscences, and leave nothing out."

"Reginald!"

"Exactly what the Duchess said when I mentioned it to her."

"They had to stop her [from] playing in the Macaws' Hockey Club because when her shins got mixed up in a scrimmage you could hear what she thought for half a mile on a clear day," said Reginald. "They are called the Macaws because of their blue and yellow costumes, but I understand there is nothing yellow about Miriam's language."

from **Reginald in Russia**, *stories and sketches:*

The Princess always defended a friend's complexion. With her, as with a great number of her sex, charity began at homeliness and did not generally progress much farther.

"In England," said the Princess, "you never go to extremes."

"We go to the Albert Hall," explained Reginald.

"I hope you will come again," said the Princess in a tone that prevented the hope from becoming too infectious.

Only the old and the clergy know how to be flippant gracefully. I was present the other day when one of the junior chaplains was preaching in aid of distressed somethings-or-other, when he remarked eloquently, "The tears of the afflicted, to what shall I liken them — to diamonds?" The other junior chaplain, who had been dozing out of professional jealousy, awoke with a start and asked hurriedly, "Shall I play to diamonds, partner?" It didn't help matters when the senior chaplain present remarked dreamily but with painful distinctness, "Double diamonds." Everyone looked at the junior preacher, half expecting him to redouble, but he contented himself with scoring what points he could under the circumstances.

"When his maternal grandmother died," said Reginald, "he didn't go so far as to give up bridge altogether but he did declare on nothing but black suits for the next three months. That, I think, was really beautiful."

Lady Anne showed no sign of being impressed. Egbert looked at her nervously through his glasses. To get the worst of an argument with her was no new experience. To get the worst of a monologue was a humiliating novelty.

The pageboy, who had Renaissance tendencies, had christened the cat Don Tarquinio. Left to themselves, Egbert and Lady Anne would unfailingly have called him Fluff, but they were not obstinate.

Egbert came into the large, dimly lit drawing room with the air of a man who is not certain whether he is entering a dovecote [bird house] or a bomb factory, and is prepared for either eventuality.

Lady Anne showed no sign of being impressed. Egbert looked at her nervously through his glasses. To get the worst of an argument with her was no new experience. To get the worst of a monologue was a humiliating novelty.

Do women ever really shop? Of course, it is a well attested fact that they go forth shopping as assiduously as a bee goes flower-visiting, but do they shop in the practical sense of the word? "We shall be out of starch by Thursday," they say with fatalistic foreboding, and by Thursday they are out of starch. They have predicted almost to the minute when their supply would give out, and if Thursday happens to be early-closing day their triumph is complete.

It is noteworthy that, just as a sheepdog seldom molests flocks in the near neighborhood, so a woman rarely deals with shops in her own vicinity. The more remote the source of supply the more fixed seems to be the resolve to run short of the commodity in question. The Ark had probably not quitted its last mooring five minutes before some feminine voice recorded a shortage of bird seed.

The directness of the masculine shopper arouses a certain combative derision in the feminine onlooker. "You're surely not buying blotting paper *here*?" she exclaimed in an agitated whisper. "Let me take you to Winks and Pinks," she added. "They've got such lovely shades of blotting paper — pearl and heliotrope and crushed —"

"But I want ordinary white blotting paper," I said.

"Never mind. They know me at Winks and Pinks," she replied inconsequently. "What do you want blotting paper for anyway?"

"I use it to dry up the ink of wet manuscripts without smudging the writing. The only other use for it that I can think of is to roll it in a ball for a kitten to play with."

"But you don't have a kitten," she said with a feminine desire for stating the entire truth on most occasions. Anyway, I never did get my blotting paper.

Mrs. Crick had a long family, and was therefore licensed in the eyes of the world to have a short temper.

"I know a little in a general way about gardening and history and the old masters," he said, "but I could never tell you offhand whether 'Stella van der Loopen' was a chrysanthemum, a heroine of the American War of Independence, or something in the Louvre."

Hating anything in the way of ill-natured gossip ourselves, we are always grateful to those who do it for us, and do it well.

Van Cheele suddenly found himself engaged in the novel process of thinking before he spoke.

Naturally Laploshka had a large circle of acquaintances, and as he exercised some care in their selection, it followed that an appreciable proportion were acquaintances whose bank balances enabled them to acquiesce indulgently in his rather one-sided views on hospitality. Thus, although possessed of only moderate means, he was able to live comfortably within his income, and still more comfortably within the income of various tolerantly disposed associates.

To have killed Laploshka was one thing; to have kept from him his beloved money would have argued a callousness of feeling of which I am not capable.

Mrs. Hoopington's shrill monologue had the field to itself. But after the Major's display, her best efforts at vocal violence missed their full effect. It was as though one had come straight from a Wagner opera into a rather tame thunderstorm.

Vanessa Peddington had a husband who was poor, with few extenuating circumstances, and an admirer who, though comfortably rich, was cumbered with a sense of honor.

Vanessa, in a way, was glad that Clyde had always done the proper thing. She had a strong natural bias towards respectability, though she would have preferred to have been respectable in smarter surroundings.

East of Budapest Vanessa's complacency began to filter away, and when she saw her husband treating the Black Sea with a familiarity which she had never been able to assume toward the English Channel, misgivings began to crowd in upon her.

Vanessa announced herself ready to follow Clyde to the end of the world. Yet it was one thing to go to the end of the world; it was quite another to make oneself at home there. Even respectability seemed to lose some of its virtue when one practiced it in a tent. Also, as the world was round, she nourished a complacent idea that in the ordinary course of things one would find oneself in the neighborhood of Hyde Park sooner or later no matter how far afield one wandered.

Dobrinton was elaborately British. He could speak of several duchesses as if he knew them — in his more inspired moments almost as if *they* knew *him*. He even pointed out blemishes in the cuisine or cellars of some of the more august London restaurants, a species of Higher Criticism which was listened to by Vanessa in awestricken admiration.

Dobrinton was bitten by a dog which was assumed to be mad, though it may only have been indiscriminating.

Emily: There's always the chance that [a child] might turn out depraved and vicious.
The Major: But good gracious, you've got to educate him first. You can't expect a boy to be vicious till he's been to a good school.

Mrs. Paly-Paget: We were packed up in a little box under the roof, and you may imagine how hot it was. Like a Turkish bath. And, of course, one couldn't see anything.
The Major: Then it was not like a Turkish bath.

Mrs. Paly-Paget: Thank you for your sympathy all the same. I daresay it was well meant. Impertinence often is.
The Major: But isn't it an exaggeration to talk of one female child as being a family?
Mrs. Paly-Paget: Really, Major, your language is extraordinary. I've only got a female child, as you call it, at present —
The Major: Oh, it won't change into a boy later on, if that's what you're counting on. Take our word for it. Once a female always a female. Nature is not infallible, but she always abides by her mistakes.

Theodoric Voler had been brought up, from infancy to the confines of middle age, by a fond mother whose chief solicitude had been to keep him screened from what she called the coarser realities of life. When she died she left Theodoric alone in a world that was real as ever, and a good deal coarser than he considered it had any need to be.

Without actually being afraid of mice, Theodoric considered that Providence, with a little exercise of moral courage, might long ago have recognized that they were not indispensable, and withdrawn them from circulation.

from ***The Chronicles of Clovis****, a book of stories*:

I wasn't living apart from my husband then. You see, neither of us could afford to make the other a separate allowance. In spite of everything that proverbs may say, poverty keeps together more homes than it breaks up.

She was looking about as pale as a beetroot that has suddenly heard bad news.

The [hounded] hyena hailed our approach with unmistakable relief and demonstrations of friendliness. It had probably been accustomed to uniform kindness from humans, while its first experience with a pack of hounds had left a bad impression. The hounds looked more than ever embarrassed as their quarry paraded its sudden intimacy with us, and the faint toot of a horn in the distance was seized on [by them] as a welcome signal for an unobtrusive departure.

"Well, we can't stay here all night with a hyena," she said.

"I don't know what your ideas of comfort are," [he replied], "but I shouldn't think of staying here all night even without a hyena."

"Merciful heaven," screamed Constance, "what on earth shall we do?"

[Clovis is] perfectly certain that at the Last Judgment Constance will ask more questions than any of the examining Seraphs.

Constance is one of those strapping, florid girls that go so well with autumn scenery or Christmas decorations in church.

When the hyena joined us again, after an absence of a few minutes, there was an air of understanding about him, as though he knew that he had done something of which we disapproved [devouring a stray gypsy child], but which he felt to be thoroughly justifiable.

"How can you let that ravenous beast trot by your side?" asked Constance.

"In the first place, I can't prevent it," [he said], "and in the second place, whatever he may be, I doubt if he's ravenous at the moment."

The gypsies were unobtrusive over their missing offspring. I don't suppose in large encampments they really know to the [nearest] child how many they've got.

The lady hailed the return of her lover with even more relief than had been occasioned by his departure.

"All decent people live beyond their means nowadays," quipped Clovis, "and those who aren't respectable live beyond the means of others. A few gifted individuals manage to do both."

"You ought not to joke about such things [health food enthusiasts]," Clovis commented. "There really are such people. To think of all the adorable things there are to eat in the world, and then go through life munching sawdust and being proud of it."

"Like the Flagellants of the Middle Ages, who went about mortifying themselves."

"They had an excuse," said Clovis. "They did it to save their immortal souls, didn't they? You needn't tell me that a man who doesn't love oysters and asparagus and good wines has got a soul, or a stomach either. He's simply got the instinct for being unhappy highly developed."

The clock struck eleven with the respectful unobtrusiveness of one whose mission in life is to be ignored.

"The crisis came," Clovis explained, "when [my mother] suddenly wanted me to be in by one o'clock every night. Imagine that sort of thing for me, who was eighteen on my last birthday."

"On your last two birthdays, to be exact."

"Well," continued Clovis, "that's not my fault. I'm not going to arrive at nineteen as long as my mother remains at thirty-seven. One must have some regard for appearances."

"I think oysters are more beautiful than any religion," Clovis said. "They not only forgive our unkindness to them. Once they arrive at the table they seem to enter thoroughly into the spirit of the thing. There's nothing in Christianity or Buddhism that quite matches the sympathetic unselfishness of an oyster."

His exterior did not suggest the sort of man in whom women are willing to pardon a generous measure of mental deficiency.

"What do you think of human intelligence?" asked Mavis Pellington lamely.

"Of whose intelligence?" asked Tobermory [a pet cat that has learned to speak].

"Oh, well, mine for instance," said Mavis with a feeble laugh.

"You put me in an embarrassing position," said Tobermory, whose tone and attitude certainly did not suggest a shred of embarrassment. "When your inclusion in this house party was suggested, Sir Wilfred protested that you were the most brainless woman of his acquaintance, and that there was a wide distinction between hospitality and the care of the feeble-minded. Lady Blemley replied that your lack of brain-power was the precise quality which had earned you your invitation, as you were the only person she could think of who might be idiotic enough to buy their old car. You know, the one they call 'The Envy of Sisyphus,' because it goes quite nicely uphill if you push it."

Lady Blemley's protestations would have had greater effect if she had not casually suggested to Mavis only that morning that the car in question would be just the thing for her down at her Devonshire home.

Major Barfield plunged in heavily to effect a diversion. "How about your [Tobermory's] carryings-on with the puss at the stables, eh?"

The moment he had said it everyone realized the blunder.

"One does not usually discuss these matters in public," said Tobermory frigidly. "From a slight observation of your ways since you've been in this house I should imagine you'd find it inconvenient if I were to shift the conversation onto your own little affairs."

The panic which ensued was not confined to the major.

"Adelaide!" said Mrs. Cornett, "do you mean to encourage that cat to go out and gossip about us in the servant's hall?"

Clovis had the presence of mind to maintain a composed exterior; privately he was calculating how long it would take to procure a box of mice as hush money.

"Why did I ever come down here," asked Agnes Resker dramatically.

Tobermory immediately accepted the opening. "Judging by what you said to Mrs. Cornett on the croquet lawn yesterday, you were out of food. You described the Blemleys as the dullest people to stay with that you knew, but said they were clever enough to employ a first-rate cook; otherwise they'd find it difficult to get anyone to come down a second time."

"There's not a word of truth in it! I appeal to Mrs. Cornett —" exclaimed Agnes.

"Mrs. Cornett repeated your remark afterwards to Bertie van Tahn," continued Tobermory, "and said, 'That woman is a regular Hunger Marcher; she'd go anywhere for four square meals a day.' And Bertie van Tahn said —"

At this point the chronicle mercifully ceased. Tobermory had glimpsed the big Tomcat from the rectory outside. In a flash he had vanished out the open French window.

* * *

Tobermory had been Cornelius Appin's [an animal trainer] one successful pupil, and he was destined to have no successor. A few weeks later an elephant in the Dresden Zoological Garden, which had shown no previous signs of irritability, broke loose and killed [Mr. Appin].

"If he was trying German irregular verbs on the poor beast," said Clovis, "he deserved all he got."

In a world that is supposed to be chiefly swayed by hunger and by love, Mrs. Packletide was an exception. Her movements and motives were largely governed by a dislike of Leona Bimberton.

She frowned at a piece of toast and ate it very slowly, as though she wished to convey the impression that the process hurt her more than it hurt the toast.

The censorious said she slept in a hammock and understood Yeats' poems, but her family denied both stories.

The cook was a great believer in the influence of environment, and nourished an obstinate conviction that if you brought rabbit and curry powder together in one dish a rabbit curry would be the result.

Mrs. De Ropp would never have confessed to herself that she disliked Conradin, though she might have been dimly aware that thwarting him 'for his own good' was a duty which she did not find particularly irksome.

His mother lived in Bethnal Green, which was not altogether his fault. One can discourage too much history in one's family, but one cannot always prevent geography.

By insisting on having your bottle pointing to the north when the cork is being drawn, and calling the waiter [by his first name], you may induce an impression on your guests which hours of labored boasting might be powerless to achieve.

I love Americans, but not when they try to speak French. What a blessing it is that they never try to speak English.

Champignons, which even a purist for Saxon English would have hesitated to address as mushrooms, had contributed their languorous, atrophied bodies to the garnishing.

"Does it?" asked the Baroness, not by way of questioning the statement, but with a painstaking effort to talk intelligently. It was the one matter in which she attempted to override the decrees of Providence, which had obviously never intended that she should talk otherwise than inanely.

"I don't know why I shouldn't talk cleverly," she would complain. "My mother was considered a brilliant conversationalist."

"These things have a way of skipping a generation," he said.

"Well, I don't think your profile is as perfect as all that," said the Baroness.

"It would be surprising if it wasn't," he replied. "My mother was one of the noted classical beauties of her day."

"These things sometimes skip a generation, you know," put in the Baroness, with the breathless haste of one to whom repartee comes as rarely as the finding of a gold-handled umbrella.

It is the safeguard of genius that it computes itself by troy weight in a world that measures by vulgar hundredweights.

"Your husband isn't a prominent Nonconformist, but his mother came of Wesleyan stock, and you must allow the newspapers some latitude," said Clovis.

Clovis was already rather bored with the story, but Mrs. Momeby was equipped with that merciless faculty which finds as much joy in the ninetieth telling as in the first.

"Is he glad to get back to Daddy and Mummy again?" crooned Mrs. Momeby. The preference which the child was showing for its [present] distractions was so marked that the question struck Clovis as being unnecessarily tactless.

Whenever a massacre of Armenians is reported from Asia Minor, everyone assumes that it has been carried out 'under orders.' No one seems to think that there are people who might *like* to kill their neighbors now and then.

Once the womenfolk discovered that it [the breakfast food 'Filboid Studge'] was thoroughly unpalatable, their zeal in forcing it on their household knew no bounds.

Filboid Studge had become a household word, but its supremacy would be challenged as soon as some yet more unpalatable food should be put on the market. There might even be a reaction in favor of something appetizing.

She looked on the country [life] as something excellent and wholesome, which was apt to become troublesome if you encouraged it overmuch.

Outside the morning room windows was a triangular slope of turf, which the indulgent might call a lawn.

She said it with the conscious air of defiance that a waiter adopts in announcing that the cheapest-priced claret on the wine list is no more.

"This story happened long ago," Clovis said, "in those uncomfortable times when one third of the people were Pagan, one third Christian, and the biggest third of all followed whichever religion the [Royal] Court happened to profess."

He had that princely gift [. . .] of being able to walk smilingly and financially unscathed through a charity bazaar, and meet the organizers next day with a solicitous 'had I but known you were in need of funds' air that is really rather a triumph of audacity.

It was one of those exuberant peaches that meet you half way, so to speak, and are all over you in a moment.

"Who are those depressed-looking young women?" asked the Baroness. "They have the look of people who've bowed to destiny and are not quite sure whether the salute will be returned. I'm always having depressing experiences, myself, but I never give them outward expression. It's as bad as looking one's age."

"With a name of that sort [Tarrington]," said Clovis, "you could raise a troop in a moment of national emergency. 'Tarrington's Light Horse' would sound quite appropriate and pulse-quickening; whereas if you were called Spoopin, for instance, the thing would be out of the question."

"My aunt never lunches," said Clovis. "In fact, she belongs to the National Anti-Luncheon League, which is doing quite a lot of good work in a quiet, unobtrusive way. A subscription of half a crown per quarter entitles you to go without ninety-two luncheons."

"I put it down the neck of a young man," said Clovis. "I told him it was a scorpion, and from the way he screamed he evidently believed it, though where the silly kid imagined I could procure a live scorpion at a garden party I don't know."

"One of the chief reasons why there are so few really great poems about Russia," explained Clovis, "is that you can't possibly get a rhyme for names like Smolensk."

Lady Susan disapproved of many things; some people would say she disapproved of most things. Disapproval was to her what neuralgia and needlework are to other women. It's not that she was particularly strict or narrow in her views, but she had been the eldest sister of a large family of self-indulgent children, and her particular form of indulgence had consisted of openly disapproving of the foibles of others.

She shut her mouth with the resolute finality of one who enjoys the blessed certainty of being implored to open it again.

"To think that a scandal of this sort should be going on under my roof!" said Mrs. Riversedge indignantly.
    "I wonder why it is that scandal seems so much worse under a roof," observed Clovis. "I've always regarded it as a proof of the superior delicacy of the cat that it conducts most of its scandals above the slates [on the roof]."

"Cobras gloat naturally," said Clovis, "just as wolves are always ravenous from mere force of habit, even after they've hopelessly overeaten themselves."

"Mr. Spabbink plays Liszt like an angel," was the hostess's enthusiastic testimonial.

"He may play him like a trout for all I care," was Groby's mental comment, "but I bet that he snores. He's just the sort and shape that would. And if I hear it through those ridiculous thin-paneled walls, there'll be trouble."

He did, and there was.

Groby stood it for about two minutes, and then made his way through the corridor into Spabbink's room. Under Groby's vigorous measures, the musician's flabby, redundant figure sat up in a bewildered semi-consciousness like an ice-cream that has been taught to beg. Groby prodded him into complete wakefulness [until] the pianist fairly lost his temper and slapped his domineering visitant. In another moment Spabbink was being nearly stifled and very effectively gagged by a pillowcase tightly bound round his head, while his plump pajama'd limbs were hauled out of bed and smacked, pinched, kicked, and bumped in a catch-as-catch-can progression across the floor, towards the shallow bath in whose utterly inadequate depths Groby perseveringly strove to drown him. For a few moments the room was almost in darkness: Groby's candle had overturned in an early stage of the scuffle, and its flicker scarcely reached to the spot where splashings, smacks, muffled cries, splutterings, and a chatter of ape-like rage told of the struggle that was being waged on the shores of the bath. A few instances later the one-sided combat was brightly lit up by the flare of blazing curtains and rapidly kindled paneling.

When the hastily aroused members of the house party stampeded out onto the lawn, the Georgian wing was well alight and belching forth masses of smoke, but some moments elapsed before Groby appeared with the half-drowned pianist in his arms, having thought of the superior drowning facilities offered by the pond at the bottom of the lawn. The cool air sobered his rage, and when he found that he was innocently acclaimed as the heroic rescuer of poor Leonard Spabbink, and loudly commended for his presence of mind in tying a wet cloth round his head to protect him from smoke suffocation, he accepted the situation, and subsequently gave a graphic account of his finding the musician asleep with an overturned candle by his side and the conflagration well started.

Spabbink gave *his* version some days later, when he had partially recovered from the shock of his midnight castigation and immersion, but the gentle pitying smiles and evasive comments with which his story was greeted warned him that the public ear was not at his disposal. He refused, however, to attend the ceremonial presentation [to Mr. Groby] of the Royal Humane Society's life-saving medal.

*from **Beasts and Super-Beasts**, a book of stories*:

Leonard Blister's beliefs were for the "few," that is to say, anyone who would listen to him.

Blister was one of those people who have failed to find this world attractive or interesting, and who have sought compensation in an "unseen world" of their own experience or imagination — or invention. Children do that sort of thing successfully, but children are content to convince themselves, and do not vulgarize their beliefs by trying to convince other people.

"I wish you would turn me into a wolf, Mr. Blister," said Mary, "a she-wolf of course. It would be too confusing to change one's sex as well as one's species at a moment's notice. Only don't do it today; we have only eight available bridge players, and it would break up one of our tables."

Insanity [in her family]? No, I never heard of any. Her father lives in West Kensington, but I believe he is sane on all other subjects.

"You are not really dying, are you?" asked Amanda.
    "I have the doctor's permission to live till Tuesday," said Laura.

"Personally, I think an otter's life would be rather enjoyable," continued Laura. "Salmon to eat all the year round, and the satisfaction of being able to fetch trout in their own homes without having to wait for hours till they condescend to rise to the fly you've dangled before them."

"Shoo! Hish! Shoo!" cried the ladies in chorus [to the large boar-pig confronting them].

"If they think they're going to drive it away by reciting a list of the kings of Israel they're laying themselves out for disappointment," observed Matilda from her seat in the tree.

"You mean *une bête*," corrected Matilda. "A pig is masculine as long as you call it a pig; but if you lose your temper and call it a ferocious beast it becomes one of us at once. French is a dreadfully unsexing language."

"Shall I recite to you to make the time pass quicker?" said Matilda [to the cornered ladies]. "*Belinda, the Little Breadwinner*, is considered my best piece. Or perhaps it ought to be something in French. But *Henri Quatre's Address to His Soldiers* is the only thing I really know in that language."

[The boar-pig] had been named Berserker in the earlier stages of its career; it was rechristened the Brogue [a heavy leather shoe] later on, in recognition of the fact that, once acquired, it was extremely difficult to get rid of. The unkinder wits of the neighborhood had been known to suggest that the first letter of the new name was superfluous.

Anyhow, he needn't have gone on about it for the entire evening and then said, "Let's say no more about it" just when I was beginning to enjoy the discussion.

"I told him that [the wild horse] was as gentle as a lamb. After all, lambs go kicking and twisting about as if they were demented, don't they?"
    "The lamb has an entirely unmerited character for sedateness," agreed Clovis.

Each of them feels that she has nursed a viper in her bosom, and nothing fans the flames of human resentment so much as the discovery that one's bosom has been utilized as a snake sanatorium.

I am told that the letters which passed between the two women were a revelation as to how much invective could be got onto a sheet of notepaper.

"It's a most awkward situation," said Mrs. Sangrail. "Do you suppose they won't speak to one another?"

"On the contrary," said Clovis, "the difficulty will be to get them to leave off. Their remarks on each other's conduct and character have hitherto been governed by the fact that only four ounces of plain speaking can be sent through the post at a time."

As a child he had been precociously brilliant, and though he could not claim to have originated the Futurist movement in literature, his *Letters to a Possible Grandson*, written at the age of fourteen, had attracted considerable notice.

A force of [replacements] was dispatched to Regent's Park to take over the duties of the striking zoo workers, chiefly at the request of the First Lord of the Admiralty, who was keenly desirous of an opportunity for performing some personal act of unobtrusive public service within the province of his department.

"If he [the First Lord of the Admiralty] insists on feeding the infant jaguar himself, in defiance of its mother's wishes, there may be need for another by-election in the north," said one of his colleagues, with a hopeful inflection in his voice. "By-elections are not very desirable at present, but we must not be selfish."

"But he [a servant] might kill me at any moment," protested Jane.

"Not at any moment," put in Clovis, "he's busy with the silver this afternoon."

The Duke of Falvertoon was one of those human hors d'oeuvres that stimulate the public appetite for sensation without giving it much to feed on.

"We got very satisfactory references about you from Canon Teep," observed Mrs. Quabarl. "A very estimable man, I should think."

"Drinks like a fish and beats his wife, otherwise a very loveable character," said [Lady Carlotta, pretending to be] the governess.

"My *dear* Miss Hope! I trust you are exaggerating," exclaimed Mrs. Quabarl.

"One must in justice admit that there is some provocation," continued the faux governess. "Mrs. Teep is quite the most irritating bridge player that I have ever sat down with; her leads and declarations would condone a certain amount of brutality in her partner, but to douse one with the contents of the only soda-water syphon in the house on a Sunday afternoon, when one couldn't get another, argues an indifference to the comfort of others which I cannot altogether overlook."

She was one of those imperfectly self-assured individuals who are magnificent and autocratic as long as they are not seriously opposed.

To be exact, you told me that [the potato] weighed just under two pounds, but I took into account the fact that homegrown vegetation and freshwater fish have an afterlife in which growth is not arrested.

She was a charming woman, and quite as intelligent as she had any need to be, but she always reminded me of some cook's idea of a Madras curry.

Lucas was an over-nourished individual with a coloring that would have been accepted as a sign of culture in an asparagus, but probably meant in this case mere abstention from exercise.

"There is no outlet for demonstrating your feelings towards people you simply loathe," said Clovis. "Just think how jolly it would be if a recognized day were set apart for the paying off of old scores and grudges, a day when one could be gracefully vindictive to a treasured list of people who must not be let off."

His hairline and forehead furnished a recessional note in a personality that was in all other respects obtrusively assertive.

Cyprian carried with him through life the wondering look of a dreamer who sees things that are not visible to ordinary mortals, and invests the commonplace things of this world with qualities unsuspected by most [with] the eyes of a poet or a real estate agent.

"What I don't see," said Clovis, "is how you will ever manage to propose to her. In all the time I have known her I don't remember her to have stopped talking for three consecutive minutes. You'll have to race her six times round the grass paddock and then blurt your proposal out before she's got her wind back."

"My mother never bothered about bringing me up," said Clovis. "She just saw to it that I got whacked at decent intervals and was taught the difference between right and wrong. There is some difference, you know, but I've forgotten what it is."

Eleanor spoke with the assured air of one who has few ideas and makes the most of them.

His cousin's aunt, who insisted, by an unwarranted stretch of the imagination, in styling herself his aunt also, had hastily invented [a thrilling] expedition in order to impress on Nicholas the delights that he had forfeited by his disgraceful conduct at the breakfast table. It was her habit, whenever one of the children fell from grace, to improvise something of a festival nature from which the offender would be rigorously barred. If all the children sinned collectively they were suddenly informed of a circus in a neighboring town, a circus of unrivalled merit and uncounted elephants, to which, but for their depravity, they would have been taken that very day.

"You are not to go in the gooseberry garden," said the aunt.

"Why not?" demanded Nicholas.

"Because you are in disgrace," said the aunt loftily.

Nicholas did not admit the flawlessness of the reasoning; he felt perfectly capable of being in disgrace *and* in the gooseberry garden at the same moment.

"Who's calling?" Nicholas asked [his aunt].

"Me," came the answer from the other side of the wall. "Didn't you hear me? I've been looking for you in the gooseberry garden, and I've slipped into the rainwater tank. Luckily there's no water in it, but the sides are slippery and I can't get out. Fetch the little ladder from under the cherry tree."

"I was told I wasn't to go into the gooseberry garden" said Nicholas promptly.

"I told you not to, and now I tell you that you may," came the voice from the rainwater tank, rather impatiently.

"Your voice doesn't sound like Aunt's," objected Nicholas. "You may be the Evil One tempting me to be disobedient. Aunt often tells me that the Evil One tempts me and that I always yield. This time I'm not going to."

"Don't talk nonsense," said the prisoner in the tank. "Go and fetch the ladder."

"Will there be strawberry jam for tea?" asked Nicholas innocently.

"Certainly there will be," said the aunt, privately resolving that Nicholas should have none of it.

"Now I know that you are the Evil One and not my aunt," shouted Nicholas gleefully. "When we asked aunt for strawberry jam yesterday, she said there wasn't any. Oh, Devil, you *have* sold yourself!"

There was an unusual sense of luxury in being able to talk to an aunt as though one were speaking to the Evil One, but Nicholas knew, with childish discernment, that such luxuries were not to be over-indulged in. He walked noisily away, and it was the kitchen maid, in search of parsley, who eventually rescued the aunt from the rainwater tank.

The aunt-by-assertion was one of those persons who think that things spoil by use and thus consign them to the dust and damp by way of preserving them.

His home was in a park-like villa-dotted district that only just escaped the reproach of being suburban.

[The artist's] "Noontide Peace," a study of two dun cows under a walnut tree, was followed by "A Midday Sanctuary," a study of a walnut tree and two dun cows.

The elk browsed in solitary aloofness in the park. It was 'tame' only in the sense that it had long ago discarded any vestige of fear of the human race; nothing in its history had encouraged its human neighbors to feel a reciprocal confidence.

The artistic groups that gathered at the little restaurant contained so many women with short hair and so many young men with long hair, who supposed themselves to be abnormally gifted in the domain of music, poetry, painting, or stagecraft, with little or nothing to support the supposition, that a self-proclaimed genius of any sort in their midst was inevitably suspect.

The sacrifices of friendship were beautiful in her eyes, as long as she was not asked to make them.

My uncle came across a giant trout in a pool just off the main stream near Ugworthy. He tried it with every kind of fly and worm for three weeks without an atom of success, and then Fate intervened on his behalf. There was a low stone bridge just over this pool, and on the last day of his fishing holiday a motor van ran violently into the parapet and turned completely over, pitching its entire load into the water. In a couple of minutes the giant trout was flapping and twisting on the bare mud at the bottom of the now-waterless pool, and my uncle was able to walk down to him and fold him to his breast. The van-load consisted of blotting paper, which had sucked up every drop of water in the pool.

from ***The Toys of Peace***, *a story collection*:

Fortunately, I didn't go to any place of devotion, though I did get mixed up with a Salvation Army procession. Interesting how they used to go about unkempt and disheveled, in a smiling rage with the world, and now they're spruced and flamboyantly decorative, like a geranium bed with religious convictions.

Neither man was talkative. And each was grateful to the other for not being talkative. That is why, from time to time, they talked.

Harvey pointed out a little lead figure of a man in black clothes. "That," he said, "is the distinguished citizen, John Stuart Mills. He was an authority on political economy."

"Why?" asked Bertie.

"Well, he wanted to be. He thought it was a useful thing to be."

Bertie gave an expressive grunt, conveying his opinion that there was no accounting for tastes.

"And that is a model of the Manchester branch of the Young Women's Christian Association," said Harvey.

"Are there any lions?" asked Eric hopefully. He had been reading Roman History and thought that where you found Christians you might reasonably be expected to find lions.

"There are no lions," said Harvey. "Now this box with a slit in it is a ballot-box. Votes are put into it at election times."

"What's put into it at other times?" asked Bertie.

"Nothing," sighed Harvey. "And this seems to be another municipal dustbin — no, I see it is a model of a school of art and a public library."

The quagmire seemed to have learned the rare art of giving way at all points without yielding an inch.

He admired a great many women collectively and dispassionately without singling out one for special matrimonial consideration, just as one might admire the Alps without feeling that one wanted any particular peak as one's own private property.

Proposing marriage, even to a nice girl, was a rather irksome business, but one could not have a honeymoon in Minorca and a subsequent life of marital happiness without such preliminaries.

Some people are born to command. Mrs. Umberleigh was born to legislate, codify, administrate, censor, license, ban, execute, and sit in judgment generally.

The Umberleigh sons propounded a theory that their [kidnapped] mother might be wandering somewhere abroad, and searched for her assiduously — chiefly, it must be admitted, at the Montmartre resort, where it was extremely improbable that she would be found.

A lump sum was to be handed over to her kidnappers and a further sum of 2,000 pounds to be paid yearly. Failing this, she would be immediately restored to her family.

Mr. Umberleigh was a rich man, and 2,000 pounds, though not exactly a fleabite, did not seem an extravagant price to pay for the boarding out of his wife.

"We shall hang her in chains over a slow fire," said one of the boys. Evidently they had been reading English history.

"Then let the pigs devour every bit of her except the palms of her hands," said another boy. It was also evident that they had been reading Biblical history.

"We shall be very sorry when we've killed Olivia," said a girl, "but we can't be sorry till we've done it."

"Come, Teddie, it's time you were in your little bed," said Luke Steffink to his son.

"That's where we all ought to be," said Mrs. Steffink.

"There wouldn't be room," said Bertie.

Presently two ominous pops, in quick succession, made themselves distinctly heard.

"They've got at the champagne!" said Mrs. Steffink [from their hiding place].

"Perhaps it's only the sparkling Moselle," said her husband hopefully.

At the age of twenty-eight, Alethia Debchance could look back on nothing more eventful than the daily round of her existence in her aunt's house at Webblehinton, a hamlet four-and-a-half miles distant from a country town and about a quarter of a century removed from modern times.

The suffragette agitators wrote sweetly argumentative plays which showed that they ought to have the vote; they smashed windows to show that they must have the vote; and they kicked Cabinet Ministers to demonstrate that they'd better have the vote.

A woman will endure discomforts, and make sacrifices, and go without things to an heroic extent, but the one luxury she will not go without is her quarrels. No matter where she may be, she will [indulge] her feminine feuds as assuredly as a Frenchman will concoct soup in the waste of the Artic regions.

Reggie listened with the attenuated regret that one bestows on an earthquake in Bolivia or a crop failure in Eastern Turkestan, events which seem so distant that one can almost persuade oneself they haven't happened. What is everybody's tragedy is nobody's tragedy.

It was one of the accepted conditions of the Rectory garden-party that four ladies, who knew very little about tennis and a great deal about the players, should sit at courtside to watch the game. It had also come to be a tradition that two of the ladies should be amiable, and that the other two should be Mrs. Dole and Mrs. Hatch-Mallard.

"How pretty the yew trees look at this time of the year," interposed a lady with a soft silvery voice that suggested a chinchilla muff painted by Whistler.

"What do you mean by 'this time of year'?" demanded Mrs. Hatch-Mallard. "Yew trees look beautiful at all times of the year. That is their charm."

"Yew trees never look anything but hideous at any time of the year," said Mrs. Dole, with the slow, emphatic relish of one who contradicts for the pleasure of the thing. "They are fit only for graveyards and cemeteries."

Mrs. Hatch-Mallard gave a sardonic snort, which, translated, meant that there were some people who were better fitted for cemeteries than for garden parties.

"What an odious young cub Bertie Dykson has become!" pronounced Mrs. Dole, remembering suddenly that Bertie was a favorite of Mrs. Hatch-Mallard. "The young men of today are not what they used to be twenty years ago."

"Of course not," said Mrs. Hatch-Mallard. "Twenty years ago Bertie Dykson was just two years old, and you must expect some difference in appearance, manner, and conversation between the two periods."

"That is where our superior powers of self-deception come in," said the niece. "We are able to live our unreal, stupid little lives on our particular Mappin terrace, and persuade ourselves that we really are untrammeled men and women leading a reasonable existence in a reasonable sphere."

"But good gracious," exclaimed the aunt, bouncing into an attitude of scandalized defense, "we *are* leading reasonable existences! What on earth do you mean by trammels?"

"We are trammeled," said the niece, calmly and pitilessly, "by restrictions of income and opportunity, and above all by lack of initiative. We are just so many animals stuck down on a Mappin terrace, with this difference in our disfavor — that the animals are there to be looked at, while nobody wants to look at us."

The mechanical toys incessantly did things that no one could want a toy to do more than a dozen times in its lifetime. It was a merciful reflection that in any right-minded nursery the lifetime would certainly be short.

From his late schooldays onward he had been possessed by an acute and obstinate form of kleptomania, having the acquisitive instinct of the collector without any of the collector's discrimination.

"Mrs. Walters considers Lloyd to be — an antelope, let us say."
   "An antelope?"
   "Well, not an antelope exactly, but something with horns and hoofs and a tail."

My dear, it was worse the year before. It was Christian Science. Selina Goobie is a sort of High Priestess of the cult, and she put down all opposition with a high hand. Then one evening, after dinner, Clovis Sangrail put a wasp down her back to see if her theory about the nonexistence of pain could be depended on in an emergency. I don't think I ever realized until that afternoon what the word "invective" could be made to mean.

I told [him] afterward that all bad feeling between the two nations had died out long ago, and that anyhow the Gaffin boy was only half French. And then he said that it was only the French half that he had been hitting.

Mrs. Gaspilton considered herself a distinctly interesting personality, and from a limited standpoint she was doubtless right.

She would like to have been the center of a literary, slightly political salon, where discerning satellites might have recognized the breath of her outlook on human affairs and the undoubted smallness of her feet.

The lesser celandine [flora] seem particularly unworthy of the attention that English poets had bestowed on it.

The Rector had not yet grasped the fact that in rural cottage life, not to have rheumatism is as glaring an omission as not to have been presented at Court would be in more ambitious circles.

[He] sat smoking his enormous green-brown cigar, without which no Burmese man, woman, or child seems really complete.

from ***The Square Egg****, a story collection*:

"Constituents are compelled to listen to all of the speeches," said the Fiend of his infernal parliament. "After all, you must remember, we are in hell."

"Nothing," continued the Demon-Orator, "is more deplorable than the tendency [of mankind] to identify fiend-hood in the most sweeping fashion, with all manner of disreputable excesses, which can only be alleged against us on the merest legendary evidence. Vices which are predominantly human are unblushingly described as inhuman, and, what is more contemptible, as fiendish. If one investigates such statements as 'inhuman treatment of ponies' or 'fiendish cruelties in the Congo,' so frequently heard on earth, one finds accumulative and indisputable evidence that it is the human treatment of ponies and Congo natives that is really at question, and that no authenticated case of fiendish agency in these atrocities can be substantiated."

The cat is domestic only as far as suits its own ends; it will not be kenneled or harnessed nor suffer any dictation as to its goings out or comings in. Confront a child, a puppy, and a kitten with a sudden danger; the child will turn instinctively for assistance, the puppy will grovel in abject submission to the impending visitation, while the kitten will brace its tiny body for a frantic resistance.

from ***The Unbearable Bassington****, a novel*:

The tea of small cress sandwiches was of that elegant proportion which, while ministering sympathetically to the moment, is happily reminiscent of a satisfactory luncheon and blessedly expectant of an elaborate dinner to come.

No one would have dreamed of calling dear Francesca Bassington sweet, but a good many people who scarcely knew her were punctilious about putting in the 'dear'.

Francesca, if pressed in an unguarded moment to describe her soul, would probably have described her drawing room.

She was one of those women towards whom fate appears to have the best intentions and never to carry them into practice.

To undiscriminating friends she appeared in the guise of a rather selfish woman, but it was merely the selfishness of one who had seen the happy and the unhappy sides of life and wished to enjoy to the utmost what was left to her of the former.

The vicissitudes of fortune had not soured her, but they had perhaps narrowed her in the sense of making her concentrate much of her sympathies on things that immediately amused her or that recalled the pleasing and successful incidents of other days.

The house on Blue Street had been left to Francesca by her old friend Sophie Chertof, but only until such time as her niece, Emmeline, should marry, when it was to pass to her as a wedding present. Emmeline was now seventeen and passably good-looking, and four or five years were all that could be safely allotted to the span of her continued spinsterhood.

Henry's talents lay so thoroughly in the direction of the uninteresting that even as an eye-witness to the massacre of St. Bartholomew he would probably have infused a flavor of boredom into his descriptions of the event.

"I was speaking down in Leicestershire the other day on this subject," said Henry, "and I pointed out at some length a thing that few people would ever stop to consider —"

Francesca went over immediately but decorously to the majority of people who would not stop to consider.

If Francesca had to listen to Henry's eloquence on any subject, she much preferred that it should be a disparagement of Eliza Barnet rather than the prevention of destitution.

"If [Comus] had unlimited money at his disposal," said Henry, "he might go into the wilds somewhere and shoot big game. I don't know what the big game have done to deserve it, but they do help to deflect the destructive energies of some of our social misfits."

"Comus has been made a prefect [at school], you know," said Francesca. "Heaven knows why."
"It can only be for prominence in gaming or athletic activities," sniffed Henry. "I think we may safely leave work and conduct out of the question."

When his sister had sealed and stamped the envelope Henry uttered a belated comment. "Perhaps it would be wiser to say nothing about the new boy to Comus. He doesn't always respond to direction, you know."
Francesca did know, and already was more than half of her brother's opinion. But the woman who can sacrifice an unspoiled stamp is probably yet unborn.

Like many boys new to a school, Lancelot Chetrof had cultivated an unhealthy passion for obeying rules and requirements.

There was a knock at the door and Lancelot entered. "I've come to be caned for missing football practice," he said. "My name is Chetrof."

"It may sound unorthodox to say so," said Comus, "but this is going to hurt you much more than it will hurt me."

"By the way," Comus said to his gasping and gulping victim when the infliction was over, "you said your name was Chetrof, didn't you? I believe I've been asked to be kind to you. As a beginning you can clean out my study. If you break anything don't come and tell me, just go out and drown yourself; it will save you from a worse fate."

"But I don't know where your study is," said the boy between his chokings.

"You'd better find it or I shall have to cane you again, really hard this time. Don't stop to thank me for all I've done, it only embarrasses me."

As Comus didn't have a study, Lancelot spent a feverish half hour looking for it, incidentally missing another football practice.

A group of Dresden figurines of some considerable value had been bequeathed to her by a discreet admirer who had added [his] death to his other kindnesses.

Eliza Barnet shared many of Henry's political and social views; she also shared his fondness for pointing things out at some length.

Serena had a way of inviting a number of men and women to her house, hoping that if you left them together long enough they would form a *salon*. Unfortunately, though you may bring brilliant talkers into your home, you cannot always make them talk. What is worse, you cannot restrict the output of those dullards who seem to have, on all subjects, much to say that was well worth leaving unsaid.

One group that Francesca passed was discussing a Spanish painter. One of her guests knew how his name was pronounced, one had noticed that there were always pomegranates in his pictures, and another knew what the pomegranates 'meant'. Francesca pushed desperately on, wondering dimly as she went what people found so unsupportable in the affliction of deafness.

"I suppose it's the Prevention of Destitution they're discussing," said Francesca to herself. "What on earth would become of these good people if anyone started a crusade for the prevention of mediocrity?"

"We were just talking about my new charge," Youghal observed genially, including in the 'we' his somewhat depressed-looking listeners, who had done none of the talking.

Francesca prided herself on being able to see things from other people's point of view, which meant, as it usually does, that she could see her point of view from various aspects.

Fate had endowed her with a son. In limiting the endowment to a solitary offspring, Fate had certainly shown a moderation which Francesca was perfectly willing to acknowledge and be thankful for.

She might have forgiven Comus for misdeeds of some gravity committed on another continent, but she could never overlook the fact that out of a dish of five plover eggs, he was certain to take three. The absent may be always wrong, but they are seldom in a position to be inconsiderate.

One cannot effectively scold a moist nineteen-year-old boy clad only in a bath towel and a cloud of steam.

Her favorite scheme of entertaining was to bring jarring and antagonistic elements into close contact and play them remorselessly one against the other. "One gets much better results under such circumstances," she observed, "than by asking people who wish to meet each other. Few people talk as brilliantly to impress a friend as they do to impress an enemy."

Lady Caroline came of a family whose individual members went through life, from the nursery to the grave, with as much tact and consideration as a cactus hedge might show in going through a crowded bathing tent.

Her pose, if one wished to be critical, was just a little too elaborately careless. She wore some excellently set rubies with that air of having more at home that is so difficult to improvise.

"The dear Archdeacon is getting *so* absentminded. Last Sunday he read a list of box-holders for the opera instead of the families of the tribes of Israel that entered Canaan. Fortunately, no one noticed the mistake."

She watched [her son's] retreating figure with eyes that grew slowly misty, and for the moment she found herself in the thrall of a very real sorrow. Then, with the admirable energy of one who is only in town for a fleeting fortnight, she raced away to be with a world-faring naval admirer at his club. Pluralism is a merciful narcotic.

I'm living so far beyond my income that we may almost be said to be living apart.

Elaine de Frey sat in a low wicker chair in the heart of a stately spacious garden that had almost made up its mind to be a park.

On a small lake floated a quartet of swans, their movements suggestive of a certain mournful listlessness, as though a weary dignity held them back from the joyous bustling life of the lesser waterfowl.

Comus for his part did not wish to lose touch with Youghal, who among other attractions possessed the recommendation of being under the ban of Comus' mother.

He preferred that people should hunt for his good qualities, and merely took very good care that as far as possible they should draw a blank. As a ruler he would have been reasonably popular; as a husband he would probably be unendurable.

In the matter of selfishness, which was the anchor of his existence, he contrived to be justly noted for doing remarkably unselfish things.

The fact that she was more than half in love with Comus made it dreadfully important that she should discover him to have a lovable soul, and Comus, it must be confessed, did little to help with the discovery.

What she tried to label as honesty in his candor was probably only a cynical defiance of the laws of right and wrong.

"You are like a relative of mine who spends his time producing improved breeds of sheep and pigs and chickens," protested Comus. "So patronizing and irritating to the Almighty, I should think, to go about putting superior finishing touches to Creation."

Whatever else you take in hand, you must never improve this garden. It's what our idea of heaven might be like if the [ancient Hebrews] hadn't invented one for us on totally different lines.

Besides being a brilliant talker, he understood the rarer art of not talking on occasion.

"Most of the really great lessons I have learned have been taught to me by the Poor," was one of Ada's favorite statements. The one great lesson that the Poor in general would have liked to teach her—that their kitchens and sickrooms were not unreservedly at her disposal as private lecture halls—she had never been able to assimilate.

Elaine had been brought up to regard Parliament as something to be treated with cheerful solemnity, like illness or family reunions.

She made a practice of unburdening herself of homilies on the evils of leisure and luxury, which did not particularly endear her to her fellow house-party guests. Hostesses regarded her as a form of social measles which everyone had to have once.

The knowledge that there was so much in the world one could buy invited speculation as to how much there was worth buying.

A domineering bridge player usually inflicts the chief damage and demoralization on his partner. Lady Caroline's special achievement was to harass and demoralize partner and opponents alike.

"I can generally manage to attend to more than one thing at a time," said Serena. "I think I must have a sort of double brain."

"Much better to economize and have one really good one," said Lady Caroline.

"Canon Besomley was here just before you came," said Serena, "you know, the big preaching man."

"I've been to hear him scold the human race once or twice," said Francesca.

"The sort of popular puppeteer who spanks the vices of his age and lunches with them afterwards," said Lady Caroline.

"He reminds one so of a circus elephant," observed Lady Caroline, "infinitely more intelligent than the people who direct him, but quite content to go on putting his foot down or taking it up as may be required."

"Some of the things he says," said Lady Caroline, "have just enough truth behind them to redeem them from being merely smart."

"One should always speak guardedly of the Opposition leaders," said Lady Caroline, in her gentlest voice. "One never knows what a change in situation may do for them."

"You mean they may one day be at the head of affairs?" asked Serena.

"I mean they may one day lead the Opposition. One never knows."

"With his prospects, he would make an excellent husband for a woman of social ambitions," said Serena, half sighing, as though she almost regretted that [her own] matrimonial arrangement precluded her from entering into the competition herself.

George St. Michael was one of those dapper, bird-like men, who seem to have been in a certain stage of middle-age for as long as memory can recall. A close-cut peaked beard lent a certain dignity to his appearance that the rest of his features and mannerisms were continually and successfully repudiating.

He lowered his voice as he spoke, not with a view to imparting mystery to his statement, but because there were other table groups within hearing to whom he hoped presently to have the privilege of re-disclosing his revelation.

It was the sort of afternoon that impels people to talk graciously of the rain as having done a lot of good, its chief merit in their eyes having been its recognition of the art of moderation.

She was decked out in the rich primitive coloring that one's taste in childhood would have insisted on before it had been schooled in the artistic value of dullness.

The farm house had that intensely English look that one seldom sees outside of Normandy.

The horse's strongest claims to distinction were his good looks and his high opinion of himself. Youghal evidently believed in thorough accord between horse and rider.

A woman whose dresses are made in Paris and whose marriage has been made in heaven might be equally biased for and against free imports.

"Are the Russians really such a gloomy people?" asked Lady Veula.

"Gloom-loving, but not in the least gloomy," said Courtenay. "They merely take their sadness pleasurably, just as we English are accused of taking our pleasures sadly."

He is studying to be a gentleman farmer, he told me. I didn't ask if both subjects were compulsory.

"Exclusiveness," said Reverend Poltimore, "has been a salvation of art, just as lack of it is proving to be the downfall of religion."

Let the idea get about that the Church is rather more exclusive than the Lawn at Ascot and you would have a quickening of religious life such as this generation has never witnessed. But as long as the clergy and the religious organizations advertise their creed on the lines of "Everybody ought to believe in us — millions do," one can expect nothing but indifference.

Lady Caroline's recollections of things that hadn't happened at the court of Queen Victoria were notoriously vivid.

It was the very widespread fear that [Lady Caroline] might one day write a book of reminiscences that made her so universally respected.

Mervyn Quentock was talking to a Serene Highness, a lady who led a life of obtrusive usefulness, largely imposed on her by a good-natured inability to say, "No."

"Do you suppose we shall all get appropriate punishments in another world for our sins in this one?"
 "Not so much for our sins as for our indiscretions; they are the things which do the most harm and cause the greatest trouble."

A misfortune of any magnitude falling on either of them would have been sincerely regretted by the other, but any minor discomfiture would have produced a feeling very much akin to satisfaction. Human nature knows millions of these inconsequential little feuds, springing up and flourishing [. . .] as a hint perhaps to crass unseeing altruists that enmity has its place and purpose in the world as well as benevolence does.

[She wore] a costume that aimed at elaboration of detail, and was damned with overmuch success.

Egbert had no small talk, but possessed an inexhaustible supply of the larger variety. He was an exponent, among other things, of what he called New Thought, which seemed to lend itself conveniently to the employment of a good deal of rather stale phraseology.

Instead of the news she was hankering for, Francesca had to listen to trivial gossip and speculation on the flirtations and affairs of a string of acquaintances whose matrimonial prospects interested her about as much as the nesting arrangements of the waterfowl in St. James Park.

"He doesn't get much opportunity for riding," said Suzette.

"What a pity," commented Elaine. "I don't think I could marry a man who wasn't fond of riding."

"Of course, that's a matter of taste," said Suzette stiffly. "Horsey men are not usually gifted with overmuch brains, are they?"

"There is as much difference between a horseman and a horsey man as there is between a well-dressed man and a dressy one," said Elaine judicially. "You may also have noticed how seldom a dressy woman really knows how to dress. As a lady of my acquaintance observed the other day, 'some people are born with a sense of how to clothe themselves, others acquire it, and others look as if their clothes had been thrust upon them.'" Although she had given Lady Caroline her due quotation marks, the sudden tactfulness with which she looked away from her lunch-mate's frock was entirely her own idea.

"He is exactly the husband I should have chosen for you," said Elaine.

For the second time that afternoon Suzette felt a sense of waning enthusiasm for one of her possessions. With a smiling air of heavy patronage, she delivered her damaging counterstroke. "And when are we to hear of your engagement, my dear?"

"Now," said Elaine quietly but with electrical effect.

A stroll homeward through the park brought her, without the possibility of escape, within hailing distance of Martha Blathington, who fastened onto her with the enthusiasm of a lonely tsetse fly encountering an outpost of civilization.

As she listened to the hostess reeling off a catalogue of inane remarks with a comfortable complacency that held out no hope of an early abandoning of the topic, Francesca sat and wondered why the innocent acceptance of a cutlet and a glass of indifferent claret should lay one open to such unsparing punishment.

"Just think," said Martha inconsequently, "my sister in Cambridgeshire has hatched out thirty-three White Orpington chicks in her incubator!"

"What [kind of] eggs did she put in?" asked Francesca.

"Oh, some very special strain of White Orpington."

"Then I don't see anything remarkable in the result. If she had put in crocodile eggs and hatched out White Orpingtons, there might have been something to write to *Country Life* about."

[She] waited with the eager patience of a terrier watching a dilatory human prepare for its outdoor walk.

It was unthinkable, but the trouble was that it had to be thought about.

Francesca's feeling toward the bringer of bad news, who sat nibbling at her tea-cakes and scattering crumbs of tiresome small talk at her feet, was one of whole-hearted dislike. She could now understand the tendency of Oriental despots to inflict death or ignominious chastisement on messengers bearing tidings of misfortune and defeat.

The theatre's stalls and boxes filled slowly and hesitatingly with a crowd whose component units seemed for the most part to recognize the probability that they were quite as interesting as any play they were likely to see.

"Who is that woman with the auburn hair and the rather belligerent gleam in her eyes?" asked a man sitting behind Comus. "She looks as if she might have created the world in six days and destroyed it on the seventh."

A buzz of recognition came from the front rows of the pit, together with a craning of necks on the part of those in less favored seats. It heralded the arrival of Shernard Blaw, the dramatist who had discovered himself, and who had given so ungrudgingly of his discovery to the world.

The Archdeacon smiled indulgently, with such saintliness that one felt that whoever else might hold keys of Paradise, he at least possessed a private latchkey to that abode.

Lady Caroline blinked her eyes. "My dear Archdeacon," she said, "no one can be an unbeliever nowadays. The Christian Apologists have left one nothing to disbelieve in."

In the front row of the upper circle a woman with a high restless voice was discussing the work of a temporarily fashionable composer, chiefly in relation to her own emotions, which she seemed to think might prove interesting to those around her.

The play promised to be a success. The author, avoiding the pitfall of brilliancy, had aimed at being interesting. And as far as possible—bearing in mind that his play was a comedy—he had strived to be amusing.

Of course, one can see the end of the play; she will come to her husband with the announcement that their longed-for child is going to be born, and that will smooth over everything. So convenient to wind up a comedy with the commencement of someone else's tragedy.

Francesca sat listening to Colonel Springfield's story of what happened to a pigeon-cote in his compound at Poona. Everyone who knew the Colonel had to listen to that story a good many times, but Lady Caroline had mitigated the boredom of the infliction, and even invested it with a certain sporting interest, by offering a prize to the person who heard it the most often in the course of the season, with the competitors being under the honorable understanding not to lead up to the subject.

"And there, dear lady," concluded the Colonel, "were the eleven dead pigeons. What became of the bandicoot, no one ever knew."

Francesca thanked him for his story, and complacently inscribed the number 4 on the margin of her theatre program.

Lady Caroline found herself at close quarters with the estimable Henry Greech, and experienced some of the joy which comes to the homeward wending hunter when a chance shot presents itself on which he may expend his remaining cartridges.

"My dear Mr. Greech," said Lady Caroline, "we all know that Prime Ministers are wedded to the truth but, like other wedded couples, they sometimes live apart."

He was one of those individuals who can describe a continent on the strength of a few days' stay in a coastal town as intimately as a paleontologist will reconstruct an extinct mammal from the evidence of a stray shinbone.

The farewell dinner which Francesca had hurriedly organized in honor of [Comus's] departure threatened from the onset to be unsuccessful. In the first place, there was very little of Comus and a good deal of farewell in it.

Argument was not congenial to his disposition, which preferred an unchallenged flow of dissertation modified by occasional helpful questions which formed the starting point for new offshoots of word-spinning.

To the spade workers who carried on the actual labor, he bore the relation of a trowel worker, delving superficially at the surface, but able to devote a proportionately greater amount of time to the advertisement of his progress and achievements.

"The gratitude of those poor creatures," said Thorle, "when I presented them each with a set of table crockery, the tears in their eyes and in their voices when they thanked me, would be impossible to describe."

"Thank you all the same for describing it," said Comus.

Like an imposing plant species that sometimes flourishes exceedingly, and makes itself at home in the dwarfing and overshadowing of all native species, Thorle dominated the dinner party and thrust its original purpose into the background.

Some women of her temperament and mentality know by heart the favorite colors, flowers, and hymns of all the members of the Royal Family. Although Mrs. Greech would possibly have failed in an examination of that nature, she knew what to do with carrots that have been over-long in storage.

He was a fluent thinker of the kind that prefers to do his thinking aloud. Lady Veula was inured to this sort of thing in her home circle, and sat listening with the stoical indifference with which an Eskimo might accept the occurrence of one snowstorm the more in the course of an Arctic winter.

Also in evidence, at discreet intervals, were stray members of the Semitic tribe that nineteen centuries of European neglect had been unable to mislay.

Elaine [made] three discoveries. First, to her disappointment, if you frequent the more expensive hotels of Europe you must be prepared to find a depressing international likeness between them all. Secondly, to her relief, one is not expected to be sentimentally amorous during a modern honeymoon. And thirdly, rather to her dismay, that her husband did not necessarily expect her to be markedly affectionate, even in private.

She rather liked the younger of the two aunts in a restricted fashion, as one likes an unpretentious restaurant that does not try to give one a musical education in addition to one's dinner.

"What I want to do is to make people think," he said, turning his prominent eyes onto his hostess. "It's so hard to make people think."

"At any rate," said Comus cryptically, "you give them the opportunity."

One felt that she would never wear more valuable diamonds than any other woman in the room, and would never be the only person to be saved in a steamboat disaster or hotel fire.

She might, as a child, have been perfectly able to recite, "On Linden When the Sun Was Low," but one felt certain that no one ever induced her to do so.

"You look more like Marjolaine than I should have thought a mortal woman of these days could," he declared. "Except that Marjolaine smiled sometimes. You have rather the air of wondering if you'd left out enough tea for the servant's breakfast."

"The telephone has robbed matrimony of most of its sting," he said, "so much more discreet than pen and ink communications which get read by the wrong people."

When one has inured oneself to the idea of a particular form of victimization it is disconcerting to be confronted with another. Many a man who would patiently undergo martyrdom for religion's sake would be furiously unwilling to be a martyr to neuralgia.

"Angels and animals would never get on together," he added. "To get on with animals you must have a sense of humor; such a sense would be of no use to angels as they never hear any jokes."

"I certainly don't think Elaine is going to be happy," said her sister. "But at least Courtenay Youghal saved her from making the greatest mistake she could have made — marrying that young Bassington."
 "He has also," responded Mrs. Goldbrook, "helped her to make the next biggest mistake of her life — marrying Courtenay Youghal."

"I think that is why you English love animals so much," pursued the Russian diplomat, "you are such splendid animals yourselves."

"In primitive days," she remarked, "I believe it was the fashion for great rulers to have large numbers of their relatives and dependents killed and buried with them. In these more enlightened times we have invented quite another way of making a great sovereign universally regretted."

from **When William Came,** *an alternative-history novella:*

She desired to escape from the doom of being a nonentity, but the escape would have to be effected in her own way. To be governed by ambition was only a shade or two better than being governed by convention.

A picnic at which three kinds of pepper were available for the caviar demanded a certain amount of respect.

The footman came round the corner with the trained silence that tactfully contrives to make itself felt.

As Cicely went down to greet her husband, she felt that she was probably very glad he was home once more, and angry with herself for not feeling greater certainty on the point.

He glanced quickly, almost furtively, around him in all directions, as would a man who is constrained by morbid curiosity to look for things that he would rather not see.

If there was an awkward remark to be made at an inconvenient moment before undesired listeners, Joan invariably made it; and when the occasion did not present itself, she was usually capable of creating it.

She was not without a certain popularity, the sort that a dashing highwayman [robber] sometimes achieves among those who are not in the habit of travelling on his particular highway.

The Divine Architect turns us out wonderfully built, and the result is charming to the eye. Then He adds another chin and three extra inches round the waist, and the effect is ruined.

He had looked critically at life from too many angles not to know that though clothes cannot make the man, they can certainly damn him.

There was a moment of silence, when he said nothing, and Joan suddenly understood the value of being occasionally tongue-tied.

Early in life Fritz had made up his mind to accept the world as it was, and to that philosophical resolution he attributed both his excellent digestion and his unruffled happiness. Perhaps he confused cause and effect; the excellent digestion may have been responsible for at least some of the philosophical serenity.

He was a bachelor of the type that is called confirmed, and which might better be labeled consecrated.

A world without women and roses and asparagus would, he admitted, be robbed of much of its charm; but with all their charm these things grew tiresome and thorny and capricious, always wanting to climb or creep into places where they were not wanted, and resolutely drooping and fading away when they were desired to flourish.

Among other things, she does an interpretive dance suggesting the life of a fern. I saw one of the rehearsals, and to me it would have equally suggested the life of John Wesley.

Lady Shalem was a woman of commanding presence, of that type which suggests a consciousness that the commands may not necessarily be obeyed.

No one could justly say that the Shalems were either oppressively vulgar or insufferably bumptious; the chief reason for their lack of popularity was probably their intense and obvious desire to be popular.

In a neighboring box sat Ronnie Storre, who was for once in a chattering mood, and an American dowager who had never been known to be in anything else.

She had a style of dancing that might best be labeled a conscientious departure from accepted methods [. . .] and swelled the exaggerated enthusiasm of the numerous art-satellites who are unstinting in their praise of anything that they are certain they cannot understand.

As he watched [the interpretive dancer] running and ricocheting about the stage, looking rather like a bird of the wagtail variety in energetic pursuit of invisible gnats and midges, he wondered how many of the middle-aged women eagerly applauding her would have taken the least notice of similar gymnastics on the part of their offspring in nursery or garden, beyond perhaps asking them not to make so much noise.

A loud barking sound, as of fur seals calling across arctic ice, came from another table, where Mrs. Mentieth-Mendlesohnn was proclaiming the glories and subtleties of the dancer's achievement. "It was a revelation," she shouted. "One just sat there and knew that one was seeing something one had never seen before, and yet one felt that one had seen it in one's brain all one's life."

To a close observer it would have seemed probable that the lady dancer's air of fatigued indifference to the flattering remarks showered on her had been as carefully rehearsed as any of her postures on the stage.

She had a knowledge of how to dress and a pleasant disposition, cankered just a little by a perpetual dread of the non-recognition of her genius.

Her remarks were framed with the view of arresting attention; someone once said of her that she ordered a sack of potatoes with the air of one who is making inquiry for a love potion.

He spoke in rapid nervous French with a northern Italian accent; the applause was unanimous. At any rate he had been brief and it was permissible to suppose that he had been witty.

Ronnie bent low over the Gräfin's hand and kissed it, partly because she was the kind of woman who naturally invoked such homage, but chiefly because he knew that the gesture showed off his smooth burnished head to advantage.

"A noisy and wearisome woman," said Cicely. "She reminds one of garlic that's been planted by mistake in a conservatory."

"The wolves which appeared earlier in the evening's entertainment, the program assures us, were trained entirely by kindness," he read in the review. "It would have been a further kindness to the audience if some of the training had been expended on Miss Mustelford's efforts at dancing. It says that the report of her fame as a dancer went before her, but that her performance last night caught it up and outstripped it."

"Today is going to be your day of triumph," said Cicely to the young man. "You've got a charming young body and no soul, and that's a fascinating combination."

That is the great secret that binds us together, the knowledge that we have no real affection for one another.

"One thing I am determined on though," Cicely said. "He shan't be a musician. It's so unsatisfactory to have to share a grand passion with a grand piano. He shall be a delightful young barbarian who thinks that Saint-Saëns is a Derby winner or a claret."

"The last boyfriend I had used to quarrel furiously with me at least once a week," said Cicely reflectively, "but then he had dark slumberous eyes that lit up magnificently when he was angry. So, it would have been a sheer waste of God's good gifts not to have sent him into a passion now and then."

She had the advantage of knowing what she was talking about, an advantage that her listeners did not in the least share.

"Do you know," said Mrs. Menteith-Mendlesohnn, "I feel just like Cortez, in the poem, gazing at the newly discovered sea."

"'Silent upon a peak in Darien,'" quoted a penetrating voice that could only belong to Joan Mardle. "I say, can anyone picture Mrs. Menteith-Mendlesohnn silent on any peak under any circumstances?"

Ronnie would acquiesce in his dismissal with the good grace born of indifference — the surest guarantor of perfect manners.

Cornelian Valpy was a fair young man with perpetual surprise impinging on his countenance and a chin that seemed to have retired from competition with the rest of his features.

"Matter?" said Cornelian. "Why should you suppose that anything is the matter?"

"When you wear a look of idiotic complacency in a Turkish bath," said the other, "it is the more noticeable from the fact that you are wearing nothing else."

Larry's father had been a brilliantly clever man who had married a brilliantly handsome woman; fate had not had the least intention that Larry, so handsome himself, should take after both parents.

*from the **Plays***:

The Baron: You would be fortunate in securing such a daughter-in-law, is it not so?
The Gräfin: Yes, Isadora has all the most desirable qualifications: heaps of money, average looks, and absolutely no brains.

The Baron: He is a clever boy, is he not?
The Gräfin: He has that perverse kind of cleverness that is infinitely more troublesome than any amount of stupidity.

Ludovic: You've heard of Mrs. Packington?
Mrs. Vulpy: No, who is she?
Ludovic: She's fabulously old, and fabulously rich, and she's been fabulously ill for longer than any living human being can remember. I believe she caught a cold at Queen Victoria's coronation and never let it go again.

Clare: A *coup d'état* is a wretchedly messy thing. It's as bad as cooking with a chafing dish; it takes such ages to clean up afterwards.

Sybil: A woman who takes her husband about with her everywhere is like a cat that goes on playing with a mouse long after she's killed it.

Clare: So many people who are described as rough diamonds turn out to be merely rough paste.

René: You ought to marry.
Trevor: You think that would improve matters?
René: Suffering is a great purifier.

Ludovic: Matrimony is not reputed to be an invariable bed of roses, but there is no reason why it should be a cactus hedge.

Clare: If Hortensia is more intolerant on one question than on any other, it's on the subject of what she calls mixed dancing. I remember a county fête where she vetoed the project of a maypole dance by children of six and seven years old until absolutely assured that the sexes would dance apart. Some of the smaller children were rather ambiguously dressed and were too shy to tell us their names, and the curate and I had a long and delicate task in sorting the he's from the she's. One four-year-old baffled our most patient researches and finally had to dance by itself round a maypole of its own.

Sybil: Why is it that plain women are always so venomous?
Agatha: Oh, if you're going to be introspective, my dear.

Ludovic: It's absurd to expect sympathy at the breakfast table. Breakfast is the most unsympathetic meal of the day. One can't love one's neighbor with any sincerity when he's helping himself to grilled mushrooms. Even at lunch one is usually in rather a quarrelsome frame of mind; you must have noticed that most family rows take place at lunchtime. By afternoon tea one begins to get polite, but one isn't really sympathetic till the second course of dinner.

Sparrowby: The future happiness of my life is wrapped up in Sybil's acceptance of my offer.
Ludovic: People who wrap up their whole future happiness in one event generally find it convenient to unwrap it later on.

Clare: As long as one marries him, what does it matter? One can afford to be neglected by one's own husband; it's when other people's husbands neglect one that one begins to talk of matrimonial disillusionment.
Mrs. Vulpy: Other people's husbands are rather an overrated lot. I prefer unmarried men any day; they've so much more experience.

René: I've no use for him; he's just the kind of idiot who comes up to you in a Turkish bath and says, "Isn't it hot?"

Ludovic: It is generally understood that a rich man has some difficulty in entering into the Kingdom of Heaven; the House of Commons is not so exclusive.

René: Personally, I am a pagan. Christians waste too much time in professing to be miserable sinners, which usually results in their being merely miserable and leaving some of the best sins undone; whereas the pagan gets cheerfully to work and commits his sins and doesn't brag so much about them.

Colonel: He comes into the category of those who are born to command.
Ludovic: Possibly. His trouble so far is that he hasn't been able to find anyone who was born to obey him.

Ludovic: Government by democracy means government of the mentally unfit by the mentally mediocre tempered by the saving grace of snobbery.

René: That's the bother of it. Ideas get used up so quickly. If the Almighty hadn't created the world at the beginning of things, Edison would probably have done it by this time on quite different lines, and then someone would have come along to prove that the Chinese had done it centuries ago.

Ludovic: The schoolboy divides womankind broadly into two species, the decent sort and the holy horror, much as the naturalist classifies snakes as either harmless or poisonous. The schoolboy is usually fairly well-informed regarding things that he doesn't have to study, but as regards women he is altogether too specific. You can't really divide them in any hard-and-fast way.

Agatha: Frankly, I consider these milk and egg statistics that one is expected to talk about in the country border on the indelicate. If I were a cow or hen, I should resent having my most private actions treated as some sort of Bridge game.

Ludovic: On her best behavior I've no doubt she's perfectly gentle and frolicsome. For that matter, cave bears probably had their after-dinner moments of comparative amiability too.

Agatha: It's simply indecent. She might wait till one husband is definitely dead before trying to rope in another.
Ludovic: My dear Agatha, brevity is the soul of widowhood.

Agatha: Sybil, I'm not going to upset all my plans just to suit your Bridge arrangements. Besides, you said the last time we played that I had no more notion of the game than an unborn parrot. I haven't got such a short memory, you see.
Sybil: I wish you hadn't got such a short temper.
Agatha: Me short-tempered! My good temper is proverbial.
Sybil: Not to say legendary.

Hortensia: I consider this impending vacancy to be a golden opportunity.
Ludovic: There are some people whose golden opportunities have a way of going prematurely grey.

René: Sparrowby is one of those people who would be enormously improved by death.

from **Rise of the Russian Empire**, *a history:*

The splendid profligate who occupied the throne of St. Peter was not actuated by a constitutional or professional abhorrence of bloodshed—under his pontificate The Eternal City had been a shambles rather than a sheepfold—but for the present the smiting of the Infidel seemed to him more urgent than the harrying of the Orthodox, especially since the Orthodox seemed well able to retaliate.

Albrecht, a bishop of the Russian Church, had instituted in that district the Order of the Warriors of Christ, whose mission was to convert the pagans by fire, then throng to the worship of Jesus, and teach them the lesson of peace on earth and goodwill toward men, with which His name was associated.

Excerpts from ***Letters:***

The sparring commenced at once and was very absorbing to watch, two men going at each other like cats, the one who drew blood first the winner. I was quite disappointed to see them stop as soon as one was scratched. I had hoped (such is our fallen nature) that they would fight to the death and was trying hurriedly to remember whether you turned your thumb up or down for mercy.

"Anyhow," [Aunt] said, "we are seeing Edinburgh." — much as Moses might have informed the companions of his forty years' wanderings that they were seeing Asia.

Have you thought of getting a wolf instead of a hound? There would be no license to pay for and at first it could be fed largely on the smaller Inktons [Latvians], with biscuits sometimes for a change. You would have to train it to distinguish the small Vernon boys from other edible sorts of course.

Whenever my horse hears another neigh she whinnies back, and being a mare always insists on having the last word.

One elderly lady asked me how old I was, and then obligingly showed me the height I ought to be. I told her that in this damp climate one must allow for shrinkage, and she did not press the matter.

Have you ever seen a dog bark and yawn at the same time? I did the other day and it reminded me of a person saying the responses in church.

A day or two before I left [Malaysia] I was enjoying a midday bath, when my [servant] came and announced that a big bear had been caught and was being brought up to me. I implored him not to do anything so rash but he went anyway saying, "Master bringing, yes." The bathroom is small and I knew that if a large bear were introduced there would be unpleasantness. I hastily forgave my enemies and tried to say my prayers, but the only one I could remember was the prayer for fine weather. As it happened my servant meant *bird* when he said bear, having caught a large sort of buzzard; so, I left off praying for fine weather and un-forgave my enemies forthwith.

This story treatment, set in the Garden of Eden, was found among Saki's papers:

The Serpent again elaborated all the arguments and inducements that he had already brought forward, but Eve's reply was unfailingly the same. The Serpent, giving a final petulant wriggle of its coils, slid away with an unmistakable air of displeasure.

"You haven't tasted the Forbidden Fruit, I suppose?" said a pleasant but rather anxious voice at Eve's shoulder a few minutes later. It was one of the Archangels speaking.

"No," said Eve, "Adam and I went into the matter very thoroughly last night and we came to the conclusion that we should be ill-advised in eating the fruit of that tree."

"Of course, it does great credit to your sense of obedience," said the Archangel with an entire lack of enthusiasm in his voice, "but it will cause considerable disappointment in some quarters. There was an idea going about that you might be persuaded into tasting it."

'There *was* a Serpent here speaking about it the last few days," said Eve. "He seemed rather huffed that we didn't follow his advice, but Adam and I went into the whole matter last night and we came to the —"

"Yes, yes," said the Archangel, "a praiseworthy decision. At the same time, well, it's not exactly what everyone anticipated. You see, Sin has got to come into the world, somehow."

"Yes?" said Eve, without any marked show of interest.

"And you are practically the only ones who *can* introduce it."

"I don't know anything about that," said Eve placidly. "Adam and I have got to think of our own interests. We went very thoroughly —"

"You see," interrupted the Archangel, "the most elaborate arrangements have been foreordained on the assumption that you *would* yield to temptation. No end of pictures of the Fall of Man are destined to be painted and a poet is going one day to write an immortal poem called, *Paradise L*—" The Archangel stopped short.

"Called what?" asked Eve.

"*Paradise . . . Life*. It's all about you and Adam eating the Forbidden Fruit. If you don't eat it, I don't see how the poem can possibly be written."

Eve is still hesitant — says she has no appetite for more fruit.

"I had some figs and half a dozen medlars early this morning, and mulberries and a few parsley-tops with a sauce of pomegranate juice, and . . ."

"The trouble is," said the Archangel reflecting later, "there is too great a profusion of fruit in that garden. There isn't enough temptation to go after one kind. Now if there was a partial crop failure . . ."

The idea was acted upon. Blight, mildew, caterpillars, and frosts worked havoc among the trees and bushes and herbs. Plants withered, others never sprouted or ripened. The Tree of Knowledge alone flaunted itself in undiminished luxuriance.

"We shall have to eat it after all," said Adam, who had breakfasted that morning on some moldy tamarinds and the rind of yesterday's melon.

"We were told not to, and we're not going to," said Eve stubbornly. Her mind's made up on the point.

For Further Reading

Books by Saki:

The Westminster Alice (London, The Westminster Gazette, 1902). Political satire.

Reginald (London, Methuen, 1904). Stories and sketches.

Reginald in Russia (London, Methuen, 1910). Stories and sketches.

The Chronicles of Clovis (London, John Lane, 1911). Stories.

The Unbearable Bassington (London, John Lane, 1912). Novel.

When William Came (London, John Lane, 1913). Alternative-history novella.

Beasts and Super-Beasts (London, John Lane, 1914). Stories.

The Toys of Peace (London, John Lane The Bodley Head, 1919). Stories.

The Square Egg and Other Sketches (London, John Lane The Bodley Head, 1924).

Collections:

The Complete Short Stories (Omnibus volume, New York, Viking Press, 1930).

The Bodley Head Saki (London, The Bodley Head, 1963). Substantial introduction by the editor.

The Complete Works of Saki (New York, Double Day, 1976). Includes the plays.

Biographical/Critical:

Langguth, A. J. *SAKI: A Life of H. H. Munro*. New York: Simon and Schuster, 1981. Also contains six stories not collected before.

Byrne, Sandie. *The Unbearable Saki: The Work of H. H. Munro*. Oxford University Press USA, 2007.

Gillen, Charles. *H. H. Munro*. Boston: Twayne Publishers, 1969. A study of the fiction.

Spears, G. J. *The Satire of Saki*. New York: Exposition Press, 1963.

Munro, E. M. "Biography of Saki," a short memoir by his sister, first published in *The Square Egg,* John Lane, 1924.

Appendix A

The Indispensable Tales:

The Storyteller
The Open Window
Tobermory
The Schwartz-Metterklume Method
The Lumber Room
The Boar-Pig
Laura
Gabriel-Ernest
The Sex that Doesn't Shop
Mrs. Packletide's Tiger
The Quest
The Strategist
The Reticence of Lady Anne
The Interlopers
Reginald at the Theatre

Appendix B

A Saki Nomenclature – the outlandish character names:

Lady Beauwhistle
Mirian Klopstock
Madame Draga
Mrs. Mudge-Jervise
Mrs. Nicorax
Mrs. Van Challaby
Mrs. Babwold
Countess Lomshen
Princess Lorikoff
Mrs. Chilworth
Mrs. Toop
Mr. Laploshka
Mrs. Wrotsley
Dolores Sneep
Brimley Bomefield
Veronique
Lady Thistledale
Betsy Croot
Florinda
Septimus Brope
the Duke of Scaw
Mrs. Troyle
Lord Hugo Sizzle
Cocksley Coxon
Groby Lington
Miss Wepley
Lady Bastable

Leonard Bilsiter
Sir Lulworth Quayne
Major Dumbarton
Clovis Sangrail
Constance Broodle
Lord Pabham
Lady Blemley
Tobermory
Major Barfield
Bertie van Tahn
Odo Finsberry
Loona Bimberton
Hofrath Schilling
Miss Gilpet
Lester Slaggby
Filboid Studge
Duncan Dullamy
Mortimer Seltoun
Prince Vespaluus
Arlington Stringham
Gertrude Ilpton
Sredni Vashtar
Mrs. Philidore Stossen
Henri Deplis
Miss Mebbin
Sir Leon Birberry
Dora Bittholz

Framton Nuttel
BillyYuttley
Vasco Honiton
Emma Ladbruk
Duke of Falvertoon
Mrs. Quabarl
Canon Teep
Gorworth
Blenkinthrope
Duckby
Lady Blonze
Rachel Kammerstein
Waldo Plubley
Basset Harrowcluff
Hermanova
Mrs. Thackenbury
Adela Chemping
Norman Gortsby
Pegginson
Betty Coulterneb
Colonel Norridrum
Marion Eggelby
Kenelm Jerton
Hildegarde Shrubley
Lady Starping
Lady Mousehilton
Lady Braddleshrub
Horace Bordenby
the Wyandottes
the Orpingtons
Alethia Debchance
Mrs. Bludward
Sir John Chobham

Ulrich von Gradwitz
Georg Znaeym
Emily Yorling
Miss Fritten
Miss Luffcombe
Lena Dubarri
Waldo Orphington
Reggie Bruttle
Major Dagberry
Mrs. Gwepton
Colonel Chuttle
Bertram Kneyght
Harry Scarisbrooke
Jocantha Bessbury
Gebhard
Knopfschrank
Syvlia Strubble
Mrs. Nougat-Jones
Sir James Beanquest
Throstlewing
Dora Yonelet
the Bickelbys
Mrs. Froplinson
Treddleford
Theophil Eshley
Lady Ulwight
Ada Bleek
Lady Befnal
Augustus Mellowkent
Caiaphas Dwelf
Bertie Dykson
Mrs. Gurtleberry
Teresa Thundleford

Amblecope
Morlvera
Clotilde
Hyacinth
Gwenda Pottingdon
Malcolm Athling
Lady Prowche
Luitpold Wolkenstein
Beryl Gaspilton
Baptiste Lepoy
Placidus Superbus
Moung Shoogala
the Gräfin von Jadstein
Mrs. Bebberley Cumble
Theodore Thropplestance
Sophie Chattel-Monkheim
Demosthenes Platterbaff
Monsieur Aristide Saucourt
Mrs. Mentieth-Mendlesohnn
Sir Gervase Cullumpton

Gorla Mustleford
Rhapsodie Pantril
Mauleverer Morle
Percival Plarsey
Cornelian Valpy
Hortensia Bavvel
René St. Gall
Lena Luddleford
Marcus Popham
Bavton Bidderdale
Mrs. Panstreppon

Made in the USA
Middletown, DE
12 May 2022